DOGS

Questions and Answers

by Christina Mia Gardeski

raintree

a Capstone company — publishers for children

Raintree is an imprint of Capstone Global Library Limited, a company incorporated in England and Wales having its registered office at 264 Banbury Road, Oxford, OX2 7DY – Registered company number: 6695582

www.raintree.co.uk
myorders@raintree.co.uk

Edited by Carrie Braulick Sheely and Alesha Halvorson
Designed by Kayla Rossow
Picture research by Pam Mitsakos
Production by Gene Bentdahl

ISBN 978 1 4747 2142 4
20 19 18 17 16
10 9 8 7 6 5 4 3 2 1

British Library Cataloguing in Publication Data
A full catalogue record for this book is available from the British Library.

Acknowledgements
Shutterstock: Andresr, 9, anetapics, 11, AVAVA, 13, Bobbymne, 15, Javier Brosch, 5, Ksenia Raykova, cover, l i g h t p o e t, 7, MaKars, 1, 22, Monkey Business Images, 19, SomPhoto, 21; Thinkstock: Fuse, 17

Printed and bound in China.

Contents

Who waits by the door?

My dog!

Dogs have twice as many ear muscles as humans. This helps them to hear sounds we cannot hear. They know someone is at the door before anyone even knocks.

Why do dogs bark?

Dogs bark to tell their owners and other dogs what they want. They bark to tell us they want to eat or walk. They bark at other dogs when they play. Dogs also bark when they want us to stay away.

Do dogs get lonely?

Dogs like to be with their owners and other dogs. Most wild dogs live in packs. A pet dog's human family is like its pack. Dogs do not like to be alone.

Why do dogs wag their tails?

Dogs wag their tails to show how they feel. Happy dogs often wag their tails high and to the right. Dogs with tails wagging low and to the left might be upset.

What do dogs eat?

Dogs will eat most foods if you let them. But some human food can make dogs ill. Wet or dry dog food that is high in protein is best. They also need fresh water every day.

How do dogs help people?

Some dogs have special jobs.

Police dogs track down criminals.

Search and rescue dogs find people

who are lost or hurt. Guide dogs help

people who cannot see.

Does my dog need a check-up?

Healthy dogs can get check-ups every year. A vet checks the dog from head to tail. The vet listens to its heart and lungs. The vet makes sure the dog does not have fleas or ticks.

Do dogs stay inside or go outside?

Dogs love to be outside.

A fence can keep your dog safe

in the garden. Take your dog for

a walk at least twice a day.

It's great exercise for you both!

Why do dogs sniff everything?

Dogs sniff to learn. Their wet noses know where you have been and what you have touched. Some dogs can even smell if people are unwell.

Glossary

flea tiny, jumping insect that sucks blood

muscle part of the body that helps move, lift or push

pack group of animals that hunts together

protein part of food that builds strong bones and muscles

tick insect that attaches itself to a person or animal to suck blood

vet person who cares for animals

Read more

Care for your Puppy (RSPCA Pet Guide), RSPCA (HarperCollins, 2015)

First Book of Dogs, Isabel Thomas (A&C Black Childrens & Educational, 2014)

Ruff's Guide to Caring for your Dog (Pets' Guides), Anita Ganeri (Raintree, 2015)

Websites

www.thekennelclub.org.uk
Discover facts and information about all types of dog breeds.

www.rspca.org.uk/adviceandwelfare/pets/dogs
Find out more about owning a dog.

Comprehension questions

1. Why is it important to take your dog to the vet for regular check-ups?

2. Why might a dog bark at someone?

Index